The Essays

TT
617
.F53
2010

First published in Italy
in 2010 by
Skira Editore S.p.A.
Palazzo Casati Stampa
via Torino 61
20123 Milano
Italy
www.skira.net

Printed and bound in Italy.
First edition

ISBN: 978-88-572-0721-6

Distributed in North America
by Rizzoli International Publications,
Inc., 300 Park Avenue South,
New York, NY 10010, USA.
Distributed elsewhere in the world
by Thames and Hudson Ltd.,
181A High Holborn, London WC1V 7QX,
United Kingdom.

Jay Fielden

fairway
the golf jacket

It might be said that golf's obsessive love of rules, including those that the ghost of Caddyshack's Judge Smails barks from the guidelines of any self-respecting country club – "Tank tops, fishnet tops, short-short cutoff jeans, sweatpants, blue jeans, bathing suits, or athletic shorts are not permitted on the course," intones rule 7.2.1 at Pinehurst, for instance – was first established in 1603, the year **James I, already the king of Scotland, ascended to the English throne, with golf clubs and a large retinue of fellow hackers in tow.**
A sportsman and a scholar, James turned the country into a cultural hothouse that gave rise to Shakespeare, Sir Francis Bacon, and Donne.
He also started the world's first country club, Blackheath, and did it in England, 146 years before there was a Royal & Ancient anything in St. Andrews. He also

gave the pastime – dreamed up, if you believe the legend, by bored Highland shepherds – a highborn sense of fun and elegance. And it was with him that the slow evolution of golf style began.

Golf's greatest prize today may be the green jacket, but for a long time it was a red one. In 'Those Red Coat Days,' Bernard Darwin's brief remembrance of what was once a ubiquitous sight on many a link, the celebrated golf writer wrote: "It seemed as if sudden warmth and sunshine had come to cheer us when there walked into the clubhouse a gentleman in a bright scarlet coat... **His collar was of royal blue velvet and his gold buttons were adorned with the insignia of that ancient and illustrious club.** He not only wore his coat in the clubhouse but he went out to play his medal round in it and the splash of scarlet on the green made people think how pleasant a sight an old medal day must have been when it was every gentleman's duty to appear in his club uniform." The golf-jacket tradition, which seems to have started at Blackheath, spread throughout the British Isles over the following centuries. The preferred hue was almost always red, but when it came to the buttons and the color chosen for the velvet collar there was endless variation. The breast pocket might also be embroidered with coat of arms, as Darwin's own Cambridge golf jacket was in the 1890s (in "gold and scarlet and ermine"). By comparison, Augusta National's mouthwash-green blazer with its breast-pocket insignia that calls to mind a Boy Scout patch seems in keeping with the ersatz age we live in. **The green jacket is a direct descendant of the red one, but it has lost almost all of its noble genes.**

The Masters, to my mind, is the major
of majors, but its trophy seems anything
but.

Impracticality can often be fun – or, at
least, look that way. Go back a hundred
years or so and the earliest pictures
taken of people playing golf tempt you
to believe that wearing a red coat is
one thing, but a hat and tails with a
stiff white shirt and tie? "If anyone had
put it into my mind that I could not
possibly have played in such an outfit,
I doubt I could have," Darwin, who
wore just such a uniform at Eton,
writes. "Ignorance being bliss, I thought
nothing about it and played tolerably
well."
It probably helped that balls were
then made of leather and stuffed with
feathers, and shafts were wood.
No one had any hope of cranking a drive
three-hundred-yards, anyway.

Being constricted might have imparted good form. Tails, after all, is the uniform of the concert pianist, whose athletic profession might actually involve more exercise.

As early as 1837 a debate started brewing over the golf jacket that wouldn't be settled for almost a century – the standard unit of measurement it takes, as it turns out, for anything to change in golf, including what you wear to play it. That year, for instance, a member of one club was fined "two tappit hens" for playing a round without his red jacket on.

Soon afterward, the Duke of Norfolk invented his eponymous tweed jacket for the purpose of hunting. Its roomy pockets, square-pleat back, and comfortable fit was also a good design for another country sport that also involved birdies. The bottom half of this evolving new ensemble was a pair of matching knickerbockers, whose knee length reached back to sixteenth-century breeches and whose usefulness in the overgrown and often muddy English countryside was what made them an enduring feature of the Englishman's wardrobe. Early on, knickers fit close to a hunter's body, which made it easy to cut through the briar patch in pursuit of quarry. The heavy fabrics that worked for one sport also worked for the other; **on the stormy and windswept tracks of Great Britain tweed was a sportsman's armor.** Throw on a pair of shoes with nails, as spikes are called over there, and you could enjoy two sports in one day without having to change a stitch.

The manicured precincts of golf had their own demands, though. And, slowly,

devotees of the game came up with their own version of the knickers: plus fours. With their billowy, bell-shaped legs, which hung gracefully four inches below the knee, **this oddly cool-looking precursors to shorts gave the game in the 1920s its Gatsbyesque aura.** Though I consider these curious pants to be the primary reason golf looked so good back then, I still hesitate to say it. It's not the pants' fault. It's where they came from, the answer to which can be found in one of the silliest entries from the annals of 'Man's Unmanliest Moments.'

During the eighteenth century in France, culottes, or knee-breeches, became a fashion craze among the noble classes. **What breasts were to the corset, calves were to short pants.** It was the era, Farid Chenoune writes in 'A History of Men's Fashion,' of

"silk-stockinged calves," especially in
France, quoting a champion of breeches
from the time, who reasoned that those
in Paris with "timid legs too shy to
show themselves" could simply beef
them up with stocking padding or,
even, false calves. I guffawed at what
seemed to me as absurd an idea
as a man wearing a powdered wig
and make-up.
One night soon after, I realized I wasn't
the only one who found calf self-
consciousness to be a laughing matter.
I was watching HBO's 'Entourage,' the
popular comedy about a young actor
who breaks out big in modern-day Los
Angeles and the gaggle of dudes from
his days growing up in Queens who
mooch off of him. In this particular
episode – number four from season two
– Johnny, the actor's neurotic brother,
nurses a wounded self-image after a
friend refers to him as "chicken legs,"

and spends the rest of the show sizing up the bulbous bounty of other guys, as he seriously ponders surgical calf implants. If you still doubt the power of the gastrocnemius muscle to make thin men whimper and strong men roar, then consider the uniform of the professional baseball player (or, for that matter, the elaborate costume of the matador, the Spanish epitome of macho). Are the knee-length tights and stirrup stockings worn by the gladiatorial likes of A-Rod not the culottes of our time? Removed by several centuries and an ocean from the charged atmosphere of Europe's class system, even a pair of funny-looking pants (which once symbolized the aristocratic excess that sparked the French evolution) can become as humble as a hot dog. Golf's great, **early professionals, including Harry Vardon, Bobby Jones,** and that era's greatest man of savoir faire, **Walter Hagen, made wearing pants to the knee as manly as humanly possible.** I've never seen a picture of **The Haig**, as he was affectionately called, that didn't show him resplendently turned out from head to toe. He was known for wearing foulard ties, gray stockings, white silk shirts, and black or brown spectator shoes, and, as the golf writer Herbert Warren Wind wrote, for breaking "eleven of the ten commandments."

The night before he won the U.S. Open in 1919 – his major titles eventually tallied eleven, which gives him an all-time rank of third behind Woods and Nicklaus – **he arrived at the course in a rumpled tuxedo to give his opponents the impression that he'd stayed out all night,** a frequent habit of his, usually in the company of his golf-afflicted friend, Al Jolson.

1

1 *A twenty-one-year-old Bobby Jones, then a member of the Harvard Golf Team, competes in a tournament in 1923. Later that year, he won the U.S. Open, the first of twelve majors that he went on to win before retiring at the age of twenty-eight*

2 *The incomparably dressed Walter Hagen embraces victory with his wife at the 1924 Open Championship at Hoylake, England*

3 *Sam Snead on the verge of winning the 1946 Open Championship, which was held at St. Andrews. In his illustrious forty-year career, he won every major except the U.S. Open, which he lost by one stroke in 1949*

2

3

4

4 *Golf brought the English and Scots together in 1608, when Blackheath, which became the world's most famous golf club, was founded. Members of the club were known to play the game in red coats*

5 *The American Walter J. Travis, nicknamed the 'Old Man' because he didn't take up the game until he was thirty-six, astonished the golf world by winning the 1904 Amateur Championship at Royal St. George's*

5

One photograph particularly stands out in my memory as an example of the champion's discerning sense for the way one should look before approaching the first tee. In it, a young Hagen, his hair parted on the side and freshly combed back, is poised at the end of a swing, tracing his drive with a surprised look of pleasure on his face. His clothes – a pair of parchment-colored pre-plus-four knickers with a matching cardigan jacket – are memorable for their simplicity and detail. Brown shoes are polished, cap-toed, and attractively shaped like those bench-made on an English last; **his knee socks are thickly ribbed and turned back to reveal a hand-knit Fair Isle pattern; and his jacket, which looks easy and inviting, is set off by the feature of a slightly raised narrow belt, balancing function and form** in a way that convinces me such a thing didn't ruin his round that day.

What is clear from even a cursory perusal of a Google image search of Hagen is that he clearly took great delight in the things he put on. The tailoring precision and variety suggest a worldliness and breadth of knowledge of the kind acquired by cultivating a wardrobe of quality and distinction. He would have been the type of aficionado who knew that nothing can truly have status without heritage. Fair Isle isn't just a pattern, for instance. When the Prince of Wales, an acquaintance of Hagen's, started wearing V-neck sweaters hand-knit on the small island north of the Scottish mainland, he revived a vanishing craft and stumbled upon a legend suggesting that the geometric designs, with their interlocking diamonds, had been passed down from Spanish sailors stranded by the Armada's defeat in 1588.

**Throughout the Roaring 1920s,
Vanity Fair brimmed with
drawings of men in endless
varieties of plus fours and
matching, as if a golfer could
never have too many choices
in his closet.** Grantland Rice, a
correspondent for Men's Wear, lifted the
concept to the level of a religious creed:
"It is worthy of note that practically
none of the leading golfers, amateurs
or professionals, are ever untidily
arrayed for battle. **The golfer owes
neatness of dress to his gallery.
If he carries no gallery he owes
it to his other club members.
If there are no other club
members around he owes it to
himself.** It will not help him in any
physical way, but it will undoubtedly
help a lot in terms of increased morale.
And there are times when morale is badly
needed following the entrance into a

yawning bunker or the depressed
feeling that comes after missing
a two-foot putt."

By the end of the decade, the look may
have begun to change but not the height
of the bar. "Once again," states 'Esquire's
Encyclopaedia of 20th Century Men's
Fashion,' "in the summer of 1928, the
fashion press equated smart clothes with
low golf scores, pointing out that the
golfers who turned in the best scores in
the National Open Championship that
year were the best-dressed men entered
in the tournament."
No one, alas, is reported to have played
in a jacket. What had emerged to take
its place was the pullover sweater, whose
combination of give and good looks sent
golf attire in a new direction: function.
Shirts were designed with a purpose in
mind, like the polo René Lacoste unveiled
on the tennis court in 1926; and, slowly

but surely, the country that would
develop and refine the very concept of
sportswear, decided there wasn't enough
time in the day to change into knickers,
and long pants – which could be worn
both in the office and on the golf green –
took over. What also prompted this quick
evolution was the realization that **what
you wear on the course should:
a) not induce heat stroke
and b) allow for the full range
of motion needed to orchestrate
mass and muscle and metal
on its trip toward the little
white ball.**
Golf was no longer just a game, it was
on its way to becoming the multi-billion-
dollar industry it is today, with every
aspect of the sport being reengineered
to improve your score: clubs that hit
straighter, balls that fly further, shoes
that make your walk less weary. There's
even a drink – Gatorade Tiger, which

golf's number one calls a "sports performance beverage." (Somehow that doesn't sound as game-enhancing to me as a spiked Arnold Palmer.) **Clothing, too, has long been trying to help you make more pars: shirts and pants breathe, stretch, and wick.** Somewhere along the way – was it the game's color-fantasia experiments of the 1960s? The sight of a young Nicklaus dominating the 1978 Player's Championship in a pair of mustard sansabelts? **Nicklaus, pulling off an improbable win at the 1986 Masters in a pair of plaid trousers that appeared to be bursting at the seams?** Jesper Parnevik's baseball cap with its bill clownishly turned up? **Or the 1999 U.S. Ryder Cup Team's uniform that made the players look as if a large, multi-topping pizza had**

exploded all over them? – the look of golf, unmoored from its classic beginnings, wandered into whimsicality.
By 1959, according to Ian Fleming's 'Goldfinger,' which was published that year, people often wore "bizarre clothes to the game." In the celebrated chapter that chronicles the £10,000 match between Bond and Auric Goldfinger, Fleming's description of their clothes defines the difference between winning non-chalance and pompous over-doing-it. **Bond turns up on the first tee in "a battered old pair of nailed Saxones... and a faded black wind-cheater"**; his nemesis, on the other hand, looked like he had allowed someone else to get him dressed that day. "Everything matched in a blaze of rust-colored tweed from the buttoned 'golfer's cap' centered on the huge, flaming red hair, to the brilliantly polished, almost

orange shoes," Fleming writes of the villain's slavish choice of a plus-four suit some three decades after it officially disappeared.
"It was as if Goldfinger had gone to his tailor and said, 'Dress me for golf – you know, like they wear in Scotland'." Years later, in the 1990s, Payne Stewart revived the plus-four era by wearing clothes almost identical to those Walter Hagen wore – and no one, for the most part, giggled.
But Stewart, like Bond, had real charisma, and it gave his nostalgic wardrobe a credibility that Goldfinger's so odiously lacked. Stewart, who died too soon, at the age of forty-two in a private jet accident, had old-world sartorial standards. His shoes were handmade in Italy, for instance. But he wasn't beyond making an impromptu adjustment, if the quality of his performance was at stake.

On the day of the fourth round of the
1999 U.S. Open at Pinehurst No. 2,
Stewart was ahead by one stroke, when,
warming up on the practice range,
it started to sprinkle. Something wasn't
right – the sleeves of the pullover shell
he was wearing were getting in the way
of his swing. He asked for a pair of
scissors, and started cutting.
Not once, but twice, so the length was just
right. The adjustment paid off: he went
on to win the tournament, which turned
out to be his most dramatic – and, sadly,
his last – victory. By then, Stewart was
already an icon, and the way he wore his
jacket became the model for today's foul-
weather gear, with its amputated sleeves.
**Gary Player, the game's
latter-day debonair champ,
still believes that there's
a mysterious link between
the way you dress and the way
you perform.**

"It played a vital role for me," Player,
the seventy-three-year-old South African,
told me. "When I show up at Augusta,
I have a set of clothes in the cupboard for
each day. I don't know anyone else who
does that." Explaining his preference
for the color black, Player, who does
a thousand sit-ups a day to make sure
he keeps his athlete's physique, added,
"I knew it was important to have a
signature – and stick with it. Africa
is considered the dark continent, so
perhaps subconsciously it was also a way
of paying tribute to the people of my
country."

**On tour these days, there
are primarily two silhouettes:
too big and too small.**
The former is what you might call
the Tony Soprano approach, the primary
purpose being to hide the results of
all those indulgent grazings on the

clubhouse menu. The hallmark of this look is generous, with pant-leg-size sleeves and multi-pleat pants.
The latter, meanwhile, is characterized by undue shrinkage, as if someone left the dryer on too long. In 2008, Phil Mickelson lost a significant amount of weight and traded in one style for the other. I'm a big fan of Phil's, but his preference for worsted-wool slacks in tones of gray and brown paired with workmanlike black golf shoes seems to say, "The golf course is my office."
At a real office the opposite is true, as there always seems to be plenty of guys in cubicles whose lower half says "I'm at work" and whose upper half says "I'm about to tee it up at Pebble Beach."
The confusion is also in the details. The fondness for unflattering colors persists, such as earth tones (yes, the very ones

that feminized Al Gore and his 2000 presidential campaign) and hues that one would more commonly associate with a potage (if he doesn't look like a carrot or beet, for instance, Sergio García seems to be impersonating a pumpkin). **Even golf shoes, once the snazziest feature of the game, today don't look like shoes so much as cartoon versions of shoes.** The ubiquity of the baseball cap is also a bit unfortunate to me. Is there not one other person besides a semi-retired and always respectably dressed Greg Norman who might have the courage to take off the hat of the sport that stole golf's pants? Since pro golf is also a game of sponsorship, **the players who look the best out there – Adam Scott, Luke Donald, Tom Watson, Davis Love – clearly believe that the tastefulness of**

their clothes is as important as the money they're being paid to wear them.

Scott takes such pride in his appearance, in fact, that when his contract recently ended with Burberry, he says he decided to forgo hundreds of thousands of endorsement money to simply have the freedom to do what the rest of us do – wear his own clothes.

Some things from the early days, however, seem like they might live forever. As anyone knows who watches golf on Sunday afternoon, the color red – almost four centuries after its birth at Blackheath – has persevered.

Like a Highland talisman from the 'Da Vinci Code,' it seems to guarantee victory after victory for the Chosen One.

François Berthoud
Born in Switzerland,
1961, lives and works in
Zurich. He is known for
his fashion illustrations.
Since the mid-1980s,
François Berthoud has
been mainly engaged
in artistic activities.
His high-impact images
bring art, fashion
and communication
together. He has
published books, staged
exhibitions and realized
special fashion projects.
He is a contributor
to major magazines
worldwide.

Jay Fielden *is*
the founding editor
of Men's Vogue.
He has also been an
editor at Vogue *and*
The New Yorker.
He lives with his
wife, Yvonne, and
three children in
Wilton, Connecticut.
Before fatherhood,
he was deeply guilty
of golf.

The publisher would like to thank the
following for the use of their photographs
in this publication, pp. 14–15:
1. Associated Press – Lapresse
2. © Bettmann / Corbis
3. Hulton Archive / Keystone / Getty Images
4. Bibliothèque des Arts décoratifs, Paris /
Archives Charmet / Bridgeman Art Library;
5. © Bettmann / Corbis

Picture research by Lynda Marshall

cover and back cover image
by François Berthoud